Navigating the Unspoken Realities of Grief

By Angela Renee' Barber, MSW

Navigating the Unspoken Realities of Grief. Copyright ©2021 by Angela Barber AND AB-Elevation. All rights reserved. No part of this book may be used or reproduced in any manner (electronic, photocopying, recording, or otherwise) without prior written permission from Angela Barber.

First Edition
ISBN: 978-1-7379841-0-8

Reviews

This book instantly grabbed my attention. It was very well thought out. It was like I could feel the emotions of the writer. I could feel that the situation was happening fast and, at some points, seemed unbearable. The authors' ability to make a connection with the reader was great. You could tell the author was vulnerable by them sharing every detail. It was like walking through the days with the author. I can't wait to read the full book. The first chapter had me wanting to read more. I am sure this novel will be one that I binge read. Overall, I love it so far. I can't wait to get the entire book.

Donielle Parham, MSW

This is a very intimate invitation to Ms. Barber's experience with death. Although it's a really challenging subject, I felt inspired to reevaluate my personal relationships and to question my authenticity in how I choose to co-exist in this realm with family and friends. It brought forth my own fears of losing my mom. This raw sharing of emotions has definitely reminded me how important it is to truly love in ACTION and to love LOUDLY. Many of us will lose our mother and will need to find ways to cope. Reading this book can serve as light and illumination when we each must step into the dark dance of dealing with death.

Bianca Thompson

It was very engaging and interesting to not only learn about someone I don't know and never met. It was also encouraging and made me feel that it's good to get to know people better than just small conversations because you never know what people go through or have been through. It allowed me to just sit back and reevaluate my life and the situations I have encountered and just pull from those experiences to become a better person.

Enjoli Edwards, MJD

As I read this chapter, I could not stop thinking about my own mother. She's getting older and with age comes health challenges. As you spoke about your mom, I could feel the love you and your siblings had for her (and will always have for her). You so vulnerably painted the picture of your love for your mom. Thanks for speaking on the challenges that your family went through while caring for her; so many can relate. I'm certain that your mom knew she was loved by you and your siblings! We all think we have more time with our loved ones, and then life happens. This is a great reminder to cherish the time we have with one another.

Carla E. Martin, Author of Discovering Her – Let's Start The Journey

My heart smiled at mom's response of renewed hope when she was told of the plan that would move her out of the facility. The collective effort of the family is a much-needed reminder of teamwork in a world with diminishing family values and respect for elders. Ms. Barber has been a dedicated caretaker both personally and professionally, now walking the reader through her own process of grieving as she carves out time to care for herself. The chapter was the writer's reflection of her own account of a topic that so many of us have experienced. The author does not tell you how to respond but simply validates our need to process grief.

Latoya Smith, MSW, LCSW

I feel like I have been given direct access to the author's thoughts, experiences, and emotions. She left nothing untold, and as someone who has also lost a mother, this is healing. There is no other book of this kind.

Karlyn Francois, MSW

I felt compassion for you as the author because it's not good for people to feel alone. However, I could relate to it in a different way. I felt like everyone around me was moving, and I was standing still - that created a feeling of loneliness. It also made me mindful of how I've treated people who have experienced a loss to avoid sometimes feeling awkward after witnessing their pain.

Terry London

To my daughters Jayla and Jasmine,

My mother taught me everything except how to live without her!

Girls, I wish I could prepare you, but having lost my mother, I don't think I can do anything to prepare you for this kind of pain. The truth is one day, I will be gone, and I can only hope that this book could in some way give you comfort. Know that I love you with everything I am.

To my mother Barbara Elaine Barber-Henderson

I miss you immensely! Without you, there would never have been me. At times I selfishly wish that you were still here, but I know you needed to rest. Thank you for your love, patience, and guidance as you raised me

Contents

Foreword...1

Introduction....................................5

First 24..9

Death Hits Different When It's Mama!..........26

My Mama (who was she?).....................34

This can't be real (the hospital stay)...........41

I thought we had more time....................52

The Year of First...............................59

First Anniversary..............................79

Living With Grief!..............................83

Acknowledgments..............................87

About the Author..............................95

Resources......................................98

Foreword

As a Clinical Psychologist, I have spent nearly a lifetime pursuing a more profound understanding of the many transitions we experience in our lives. We've all been there to some degree, I'd expect. Some people may entertain an existential reflection of our very existence, while others may ponder the divine wisdom behind why we navigate from one stage of life to another just to eventually and undoubtedly collide with our inevitable conclusion… death. While it is human nature for us to grapple with the very real nature of mortality, dealing with the grief that follows can feel like a long, lonely road of isolation and downright despair! I believe it takes an extra measure of courage to delve so intimately into the topic of grieving as Angela Barber does in this book. After the death of her mother, Angela sought to gain a better understanding of the complex process of grieving, and her decision to share her journey through this book was nothing short of brilliant as it seeks to help others to navigate a healthy pathway toward their own personal healing.

Angela has been my dearest friend for the better part of my life. I have watched her tackle one monumental challenge after the other throughout the years and with mounting successes! I was honored to have witnessed her epic journey through the adoption and raising of two beautiful, well-adjusted daughters (as a single parent). I was beyond impressed to watch as she worked tirelessly to build her brand and become a successful entrepreneur. I was both overjoyed and exceedingly proud to watch her conquer the massive "beast" called Graduate School while working full time and raising two children. I have been blessed throughout my years to know many remarkable women, and Angela stands securely among the best! When she lost her mother, we both knew that grief would be a massive challenge, but neither of us knew exactly what the process would entail. Navigating a path through grief would require more than the strength and courage that Angela had demonstrated time and time again throughout her life. We also knew that it would involve more than that elusive amount of time that "heals all wounds." True to her character, Angela began (and continues) to navigate her journey through grief with intense passion and a genuine quest for deeper knowledge that she employs as a gateway to helping others navigate their own personal journeys through grief.

Grief is a reality that we all will face. While there is a myriad of reactions to grief, there are some universal truths that can help us navigate our own personal experience with authenticity, compassion, perseverance, and an overall healthier adjustment. Our fundamental need for healthy adjustment highlights the importance of books such as this, and I am privileged to have been a part of this one.

India Gray-Schmiedlin Ph.D., LP

Introduction

Dealing with the loss of my mother has been the hardest thing I have ever had to go through. As I write this, it has been a year and two months exactly. I am still in the grieving process, but I decided to write this book in hopes that my journey could help others. I wanted to put on paper some of the challenges I faced the first year after losing my mother. In addition, I wanted to shed light on some of the unspoken challenges I faced and share some of the things that have helped me.

Immediately after losing my mother, I got a rush of calls, texts, emails, Facebook posts, and whatever other means of communication people could think of. I had not even had a moment to breathe, and the news was out. So many people asked me what I needed or said, "let me know if you need anything." The honest answer is I did not know what I needed. I was barely holding it together. I wanted someone just to hold me and say everything was going to be ok, someone to be there for me and let me be, cry if I needed to, or talk if I needed to. This, for me, was the worst time in the world to be single. It was hard to sleep because my mind would be racing as I thought to myself, is this real, is my mother gone. Thinking about our last conversations and the last time I had an opportunity to see her, the pain was excruciating.

I could not get lost in my thoughts and feelings; I had to make sure my daughters and siblings were doing ok as best I could. Although we have lost people in our family, this was the closest person to my daughters, who passed away. I was also trying to make sure her siblings (My aunts and uncle) were ok; it was helpful to reach out to their children to let them know what was going on so they could check on their parents.

As difficult as it was planning and preparing for the service, I faced a different set of challenges once everything was over. I remember meeting up with family the morning after services as they were planning to return to their hometowns; I was not ready for them to leave. Still, I knew they had to get back. I had heard that the real work begins once services are over and everyone goes home. That was my experience; the calls and text slowed to a stop, and after a few weeks, some people started to believe I should be over it. The truth is you do not get over it; you just learn to live with it. Unfortunately, my mother will not be here with me for the rest of my life, so I must learn to live with the grief.

Be patient with yourself, and don't compare your grief to others; it's not the same. Grief will be different depending on the person you lost, your relationship with them, and the circumstances surrounding the loss. No one can tell you how to grieve or how long to grieve; the journey is yours and yours alone. You will need to look out for self-destructive coping mechanisms or thoughts and attitudes that will not serve you in the long run. When you are ready to seek help, talk about what you are feeling. Be patient with those around you; most will not understand. This book could be helpful to those grieving and potentially helpful for those looking to support a loved one who is going through grief.

Chapter 1

First 24

That was the most challenging 24 hours of my life. We had family members in town, and I had spent the night with one of my cousins at the hotel that night. That following day, I was awake, but I was lying in bed. I do not remember what I was thinking about, but the phone rang, and I saw that it was the hospice facility. When I answered, the person on the phone asked to speak with me; I sat up in the bed and said, this is her. NOTHING could have prepared me for her following words; she said, "I am so sorry your mom passed away this morning" I am always so calm and relaxed on the outside but not this time. I could not hold it; I lost it. I do not remember what she said next, but I remember eventually hearing, "Do you need me to give you a minute? You want to call me back" I somehow managed to say yes and hung up the phone.

My cousin sat up in the bed and said, "Elaine passed"? When I said yes, she responded, what do you want me to do? I do not know if I said anything, but she went into the bathroom to get me a towel. I cannot describe to you what I felt at that moment as I fell to my knees and leaned against the bed. I wanted to stay there, but Suddenly, I realized that I needed to tell my siblings. My mom's sisters were planning to see her at the facility this morning; Then, I realized I needed to inform them before they headed to the facility.

I got up from the floor and asked my cousin to call her mother to let her know. I began to get dressed, and then I remembered I needed to call the hospice facility back. So I sat on the bed and dialed the number, told them who I was, and they began to explain the next steps. She said, you guys can come and see her before we take her downstairs to the morgue; however, due to COVID, we must limit the number of people coming in. I asked how many people we could have she said maybe about 10, but we may do a few more. She then said we are not allowed to leave the body on this floor more than 4 hours after the time of death, so you guys would need to get here soon. I quietly asked, what was the time of death? Honestly, I heard her, but I do not remember what she said. I know it was seven something.

    Oh, shit, please call your mom back and ask them not to tell anyone; my siblings do not know yet. It was too late when my cousin called; one of my aunts had already started making calls. I thought, now I will have to tell them over the phone that our mother was gone; I do not need them to hear it from someone else. Then the next thought that came rushing to my mind was, Oh My God, I need to tell my girls that their grandmother is gone. I frantically got my things together to leave the hotel. My cousin agreed to drive, and I started calling my siblings. One of my brothers would not answer the phone for me. I think he already knew, I did not call often, and on top of that, it was early in the morning. Finally, I reached my other siblings and explained that mom was gone. I told them we could see her, but we needed to hurry. I tried my youngest brother again; he picked up the phone and said, "I know, and I am not coming" he then said I love you, and I will talk to you later.

We pull up at my house, and I hesitate to go in because now I have to find the words to tell my children. I went into the house and walked into my room; they both had decided to sleep in my room since I was not home. They were still asleep part of me wanted to wait, but I couldn't because we have a timeframe. I shook their legs and said, girls, wake up. I need to tell you something, they grumbled, as they usually would. "I said your granny died this morning." I don't know what I was expecting but not what happened; they both lost it. All I could do was take off my shoes and lay down with them to hold them. I waited about five minutes and said I needed to go to the hospice facility. I wanted to give them more time, but I couldn't; I needed to call the facility back and tell them how many people were coming. I said to them; you guys can get dressed quickly and go with me or stay home. But unfortunately, you cannot go in you are not old enough (you had to be at least 18).

    I walked out of my room as my girls got up to get dressed. My sisters were in the living room. I told them I needed to know how many people were going to the facility because they only allowed so many people. We called my other brother (Kevin) and came up with 12 people. I called the facility, and she agreed to accommodate that number.

I pulled up to the hospice facility, and there were way more than 12 of my family members out there; obviously, most of whom were not in my number. I get out of the car; they have already begun going up and decided who was next– WHAT THE HELL!! Now we have a problem; we cannot get more than 12, and some who were expecting to go will not be allowed. I pulled my siblings aside and asked are you guys going up? They all said yes. I was willing to give up my spot, but, in hindsight, maybe I should not have. I was just there the night before and felt it would be ok to let someone else go. Then I had to scramble to break the news to those out there that thought they would be able to go up. "I am sorry, I know you loved my mother, your aunt, but they are not allowing more than 12 people" Of course, they were upset, but there was just nothing I could do.

I look around, and my girls are off to the side crying. I had to comfort them. They wanted to go upstairs to see their granny. I assured them they would get to see her at the funeral.

We started to get down to the last few people, and I got a call; my niece went upstairs with my aunt, and now she would not come down. My aunt said she was standing there saying, "this is just not right; they did not even try to help my granny." So I grabbed my brother and my niece's mother, and we walked to the door (we could not go up; we just waited at the door for her to come down so we could comfort her). As I am standing there, I wonder, am I part of the "they" she is talking about? I was the decision-maker, although I consulted with my siblings on each decision. Finally, she came down and fell into my arms, repeating, this does not seem right. All I could do was hold her; there was nothing to say.

My phone rings again; this time, the hospice facility says we are getting down to the last few people, and we need to give you your mother's belongings. I asked do I count in that 12 number; she said unfortunately yes. So I requested she give the items to my brother and gave her his name. So the last two people able to see my mom at the facility were my brother and my stepfather.

    My aunt walks over and says, can I talk to you for a second. As we walked away from everyone else, she said, " Have you thought about where you want them to send the body. Damn really? Can I breathe for a second! If you have aunts like mine, you know I did not say that out loud; otherwise, I would not be here to share this story. I knew she was trying to help me because she knew I had no clue. Everything just seemed to be moving way too fast for me. So, what came out of my mouth was, I have not. She gently said, you guys need to talk about it; they will not hold the body long.

My brother came back downstairs; I pulled the siblings together to asked what funeral home we would use. One sibling was adamant about a particular place, and I honestly did not care. Finally, my brother said, what day are we having the service, Tuesday or Wednesday? Today was Sunday; my mom has not been gone for 4 hours yet. This was all happening too fast for me. I wanted things to slow down just a bit; let me catch my breath. After a few more moments of gathering and mingling with family outside, we all left and went back to my place.

My sister and I had just moved together six months ago to get my mom out of the nursing home where she was living. On the way home from the hospice facility, I began to text my close friends to let them know that my mom had passed on. By now, my family was starting to post on Facebook, and my phone was blowing up. I was in such a daze I could not talk, so very few calls got answered. My text to my friends read, "I can't talk right now, but my mom passed this morning. I will call you when I can."

Back at the house, I was just numb. There was just so much going on. Some people were walking around planning what to eat; others ran to the store to get groceries. Still, others were preparing to cook. By now, many people are showing up at the house, family members and friends of my siblings. I do not think any of my friends came, they may have, but it was all just a blur.

My aunt comes over to me again and says did you call the funeral home yet? The facility needs to know what to do with the body. My heart sank; I did not want to have to think about this right now, but I knew I had to. So I called the funeral home to arrange to meet with them; they told me I needed to come in to sign for the body to be released. My cousin, "My rock," grabbed her things, and off we went to the funeral home. At this point, it almost seemed I was out of my body. There was no time to think, no time to grieve, no time to breathe. There was just so much to be done, and I had to do it. I signed the papers, then called my brother to figure out a time we could meet to make the arrangements. We decided Monday at 1: pm. It was explained that due to COVID 19, only 50 people would be allowed at the services. Although that number would be challenging, I thought we would have to make it work.

I got back to the house; we had many people over, but most were in the backyard; only close family members were in the house. I do not remember much about the rest of the day. When I went to my room to lay down, I could not sleep. I lay in bed thinking, is this real. Is she gone? It seemed like a million things ran through my mind, but I eventually drifted off to sleep. I was awakened as my bedroom door swung open, and my oldest daughter came in with a face full of tears, jumped into bed with me, and laid there crying. I lay there holding her, wondering what I could say, but there was nothing. Finally, after about ten minutes, I said, " Do you want to go into her room and find something of hers that you want to take in your room with you " she said yes. So we got up and went to my mother's room together. My youngest daughter joined us, and they each picked one of my mother's blankets to take to their rooms. I go back to bed to lay down when all of a sudden, I think about my brother, who is currently incarcerated. I began trying to figure how we could let him know before he called home. I did not want anyone to tell him without the staff knowing what was going on.

    I did not get much sleep that night; I got out of bed called the jail, trying to find out who I needed to call. I finally got to a social worker who took the information and told me she would have the guards bring him down to inform him. In addition, she gave me the information so I could call back once the arrangements were made, then he could join services via zoom.

My family comes back over to the house the next day. My aunt pulls me aside and says have you called the insurance company because you will need that information before you go to the funeral home. I go outside to call because my house is full of people, I get on the phone calling the insurance company, and of course, they cannot find the policy. I began walking as they transferred me from person to person. I'm sad, Anxious, and Angry all at the same time. I walked to the corner, then began walking from one corner to the next over and over again. At some point, I looked at the porch and noticed my aunt and cousin were now outside watching me. Finally, they found the policy and confirmed the amount. It was a little more than I thought but not quite enough to cover services.

I walk back to my aunt and cousin, but I remember they are heading home today as I'm walking. I felt lost; what am I supposed to do without them here. My aunt had been guiding me through this whole process; although it had been hard at times, I just would not have gotten things done without her. My cousin did not say much, but she was right there by my side the whole time. She was asking if I needed anything and helping out wherever she saw a need. Finally, they assured me they were coming back for the service. They told me to call them when I left the funeral home, making arrangements to let them know what we decided.

My brother and I met up at the funeral home. The funeral director comes to get us and walks us to the back. When we get to her office, I'm still thinking, is this real, am I doing this. Of course, then comes the sales pitch. Surprisingly both my brother and I kept our heads. We were not emotional, or at least not outwardly. The funeral director began to explain that due to COVID 19, we would only be allowed ten people. My heart sank, my mother has six living children, and this does not begin to include grandchildren. I told her that we were told yesterday we would be allowed, 50 people. She apologizes and says that the staff that spoke with me the day before was miss informed. She then began to show us the prices for everything as we looked over the costs; she asked if we had a minister and singer. She then added that we do have a package for that as well. A rush of emotion came over me, and I asked if she would give us a minute to talk. She agreed and walked out of the room.

I said to my brother, I do not want to do all this, and we can only have ten people. After some discussion, he agreed, and we opted to have a 3-

hour visitation. Then she took us to pick out the casket to rent and urns to purchase. After picking out everything, she took us back to the office to talk about obituaries and flowers. Once everything was decided, it was time to discuss payments. I opted to sign over the policy to them; there would be nothing left anyway. My brother paid half of the balance, and I was to return with the other half before the day of the service. She explained the process, what I needed to bring for my mom to wear, and when to get there. She also explained that we would be allowed to view and approve the body before she went out for public viewing.

Chapter 2

Death hits different when it's Mama!

I have lost many family members to death, but nothing prepared me for the loss of my mother. This writing is not intended to suggest that we all handle loss the same or should. We are all individuals with our own life experiences and our ideas about coping with loss. My mother had seven children, one leaving before her. Still, I can tell you that the remaining six have our own experience with the loss of our mother. In this book, I will share my experience of losing my mother and my ways of coping in hopes that it might help someone else.

At this point in my life, I've certainly had my share of losses. When I was five years old, I lost my sister, I was a child, so I really cannot say how I handled It. My sister's death was a life-changing experience for me; as a result of my sister being killed, my brother and I were taken from my mother and placed in foster care. My mother did what was asked of her and regained custody of us, but that is a different story. The person I lost next was my stepfather's mother. I do not remember anything about her, but I remember going to the funeral. I remember sitting close to the front row staring at the casket, staring at her, thinking I did not want to forget how she looked. I do not remember how old I was, but I was old enough to know that I would never see her again.

On January 14, 1991, I attended my paternal grandmother's funeral, Mrs. Katherine Butler. I was 19 years old. I did not meet my father until I was 16, so I had not had much of an opportunity to know her, but I mourned the lack of opportunity to get to know her. I am grateful that I still have a letter she wrote to me after first meeting her. On October 10, 1992, I attended the funeral service of my first cousin, Ernest M. Taylor. I was 20, and he was just 19. He was killed in the streets of Chicago. May 19, 1993, I attended the funeral of yet another Cousin Jerry Ford Barber; he was killed in the streets of Jackson Ms. He was 27, I was 21. December 26, 1994, I attended the funeral of my maternal great-grandmother Mrs. Lillie Bell-Ford; sadly, I did not know her well. I felt like I was losing a piece of my history; I was 23 years old.

October 2, 1995, I attended the funeral of my cousin Alethea (Lisa) Taylor. I was 23, and she was just 24. She was the sister of the cousin I lost in 1992. All of this must have been too much for my brother; when it came time for the final viewing, he walked to the casket, grabbed the side of it, and let out a cry that I had never heard. Some of my family members had to get him and practically pry his hand away from the casket. July 8, 1996, I attended the funeral of another first cousin, Kenneth Maurice Muhammad. At that point, I had lost six family members in as many years; I was 24. I'm starting to have nightmares about dying myself and losing my brothers or mother.

My maternal grandfather James Barber died in October 1997. I remember being filled with regret that I have lost another grandparent, another piece of my history, and I had not taken the opportunity to capture it. I decided that I would not lose another family member and have regrets. I will do everything I can to have the best relationship with people while they are here. We had a break of a few years without losing anyone in my family. I lost my aunt, and my mom lost her oldest sister Mrs. Gloria Ann Brown the funeral was August 12, 2006. My aunt Margrett Ford died in July 2017. My cousin Alex Johnson died in August 2018.

The days and weeks following losing my mother were just a blur. I have never been through anything this hard in my life. I could not sleep, I did not know what to do, and I could fix it. But, it could not be fixed. I laid in bed many nights, wondering if this was real. Is she gone and never coming back? This pain seemed too much to handle. I have been single for the majority of my life, and this was the most painful. Many of those nights, I wished I had someone to hold me; they did not need to say anything, be there, just hold me as I desperately tried to hold on to my sanity. I am naturally a stuffer, so that is what I began to do.

My mom passed on a Sunday; we made funeral arrangements that Monday, and I went to work on Tuesday. I did not go to work because I was ok; I went to work because I did not know what else to do. I could not stay in the house. Wednesday, I went to work, but I realized it was a mistake to be back at work and arranged to take days off. I was also in school at the time finishing up my MSW. One night I was in one of my classes that week trying to explain to my professor that I needed more time for my assignment. I did not tell him that my mom had passed away because we were in the middle of class; he was not trying to hear it. I probably would not have told him and tried to get the work done, but I had already mentioned it to a classmate, and she called him after class. He did contact me to offer his condolences and grant me more time.

I began to notice that I was developing some self-destructive behaviors. I started going to the boat every day to get out of the house. Because I still could not sleep, I started drinking every night because it would help me sleep. I guess the angels were watching over me because I was not losing money on the boat. I would lose some, then win it back, then I'd sit in the food court until I was ready to leave. Although I drank every night, I was not drinking much. I drank less than half a shot, but it was a lot for me because I did not drink often. Once I realized it, I stopped so that it would not become a problem. I am super grateful that I was able to see it.

I was sad when I lost those other family members, but none caused the pain I felt when my mother left me. I expected that all death was the same, I knew I'd be sad, but no one could have told me it would be like this. She has been gone for over a year, and still, I have rough days.

Chapter 3

My Mama (who was she?)

In Jackson, Mississippi, Barbara Elaine Barber-Henderson was born on October 11, 1955, to James Barber and Bessie Lee Ford-Barber. My mother shared so many childhood stories with me, much of it was trauma-filled, but I will not go into that now since that's not the book's focus. My mother lost her mother at three years old and, at that point, moved to Chicago to be raised by her father. At around 14, she ran away from home. She ended up back in Jackson, Mississippi, with her grandmother and 4 of her other siblings.

At 15, she got pregnant with me, her first child. She was nervous about telling my father she was pregnant. So she told his sister, who convinced her that telling him would be the right thing to do, so she did. I wish I had gotten the opportunity to meet her, but she died before I met him. When her grandmother learned she was pregnant, she said, "I do not know what you are going to do, but you cannot stay here."

Lucky for her, she had an older sister who lived in East St. Louis and said send her to me. At 18, she was pregnant with my brother. At about 21 or 22, she buried her third child, murdered by someone she was dating. Sometime after the funeral, my brother and I were taken from her by DCFS. Anyone who knows anything about DCFS knows that regaining custody of your children is not an easy task, but that is what she did. She jumped through all the hoops, and after about three years, she regained custody of my brother and me. She got married and had four more children.

    I learned so much from my mother. She was always so selfless as to make sure my sibling and I had what we needed. My mother did not work when I was growing up, so we did not have much at all. As I remember it, she had even less because she sacrificed for us. Holidays were always my favorite. We would stay up all night the night before cooking. Of course, I did not appreciate it at the time, but I cherish those memories now. When I was about 16, my mother was stressing about Christmas gifts for us. I told her not to worry about me, and Kevin (my brother under me, who was about 13) just get some things for the little kids. My brother did not appreciate me saying that, but I think my mother was proud that I could be selfless and think about my sibling.

When I was about 20, I was in college, and the professor gave a lecture about dyslexia and how there is no cure. Those that have it just need to learn to live with it. I felt sad for them, and it affected me in a way that I could not shake. I told my mother about that lecture and how I felt about it. She says you have dyslexia; I quickly replied, "No, I do not." She said, yes, you do; why do you think I used to sit with you every night to do your homework? I responded I don't know. I thought that was what parents were supposed to do. We had a few more conversations where I would express my devastation. Eventually, she said to me, why are you letting this bother you? You have been living with it all this time, and by the time you were in high school, you would not let me sit with you anymore. You finished high school, and now you are in college. Having dyslexia is not something that is going to stop you.

Well, that was our last conversation about that. After that, my mother and I had many discussions about life stuff; even as a young child, I remember her life being an open book. She would talk to me about so many things. I remember those conversations like they happened yesterday.

As I mentioned earlier, my mother had seven children (one preceded her in death), and she managed to spoil each of us. We all knew that there was nothing she wouldn't do for us if she could. I say all that to say that my mother was a resilient woman. She overcame her childhood trauma and struggles as a young adult and did the very best she could to raise her children. She was the best mother and grandmother a child could have. Her goal was never to miss an event. She was at every birthday party, graduation, and dance recital. She loved her family; if anyone needed her, she tried to be there. If someone was in the hospital, she was sitting right beside them.

I am grateful that I had the pleasure of having her as my mother. I am thankful that I took opportunities to sacrifice for her as her health failed her, as she did for me while raising me. Of course, there were times that I did not appreciate those opportunities and even complained, but I would be the first to tell you that I would do them again if given a chance. I am the women I am today because of her.

Chapter 4

This can't be real

(The hospital stay)

This is the hardest thing I have ever had to go through! I am not sure how I will get through this; I do not know what to do. Right now, I have just decided to write through the pain. First, I'll just tell you that it's only been two weeks since my mom passed away. So much of what I will be writing is still fresh in my mind and in the moment.

The last time I saw her at home was the morning of Memorial Day. We decided we were going to have a small family gathering. We put some things on the grill, and my brothers took my mother out to the backyard. It was the first time she had even been able to see the yard. We sat out in the yard chatting for a while. I did not stay out long; I typically do not enjoy time out in the grass. That evening they brought her into the house, and we ate dinner. I went to bed and remembered being awakened by my mother's emergency system. They were trying to communicate with her because she had pushed the button. My daughters were telling her they did not know how to work the system. When I got up to see what was going on, my mother told me she could not breathe and had called for an ambulance. So, the last time I saw her awake and alert was as I sat on the couch watching the ambulance wheel her out of the house.

My mom was in the hospital for almost three weeks before she passed away; for nearly two weeks of the time, we had not even spoken with her. Friday, May 29, the first surgery was scheduled. I had to call the hospital to find out how everything went. I talked to a nurse who reported that things went well and she was resting. Monday, June 1st second surgery, I called again, and they again said things went well, and she was resting. On Wednesday, June 3, 2020, I remember getting a call from My mother's doctor, who told me they needed to run some tests. He said, "your mother is very sick" he began to explain the tests they wanted to run and all the possible complications of the test. He explained what it meant if they found what they suspected and what it would mean if they did not. Although I appreciated the information at some point, I thought to myself, I have never spoken to him before; why is he calling me now. Then it happened; he said, your mother can no longer make decisions for herself; you have power of attorney, so we were hoping you could permit us to run the test.

    I asked all the usual questions; have you considered her other conditions? and how might they be affected by this test? What happens if you don't do the test, are there any other possibilities? If your suspicion is correct, what are the treatments for the condition? Etc. After answering every question I asked him, he said, I'll give you some time, but we need a decision as soon as possible. My heart sank; I had not spoken with my mother in over a week. That was not like her. She usually called all day, every day, even being in the hospital.

    I was working from home because of COVID 19; I had just started a new job six months earlier and was barely out of training. I sat back for a moment and thought, "What the hell." I became emotional. I took a moment to cry and gather my thoughts, sorting out how I felt about what I had just heard. I got myself together then called my brother (Kevin), the one under me, to tell him what the doctor said and get his thoughts. I called my other siblings, and my aunts then decided to have the test done. They did not find what they thought they would find, but the doctor said very plainly, "your mother is very sick," at this point, we do not know what is wrong, but we will keep looking. To some degree, I was relieved to know that whatever it was, they suspected they did not find it. I honestly cannot even remember right now what it was. I asked the doctor if we could come and see her. He said they have many restrictions because of COVID 19, so I do not think they are allowing visitors, but I will put you in touch with the person handling that. I spoke with them they said we are only allowing a one-time visit, for one hour, and only one person. I thought, ok, well it's something, but who gets to go?

My mother has six children, not to mention her three sisters and one brother. Well, it would be one of the children but who. I made calls to my siblings, and my youngest brother decided it was him and he was about to be on his way. I convinced him to wait because this was a one-time visit, so should we use it now or wait until she is more awake and knows you are there. More importantly, this needed to be a group decision. You cannot just decide; it's you. That did not go over well, and he said, fine, just take me out of the messages then. The second oldest and I had decided that we would take ourselves out of it, but now we were down to three. So I called the hospital again to ask if there was any way we could have three people visit 20 minutes each during that one hour. They said no and repeated it's one visit, one hour, one person. Then she called it an "End of Life visit." I thought, wait, what? End of life visit! I got off the phone in a dazed as if someone had just sucker-punched me. Anybody who knows me knows that I feel deeply, but nobody would ever know it while I'm going through it. I mask everything; sometimes, I even fool myself. I took a minute to cry and get myself together. Then I called my sibling and Aunt to give them the news. They ran another test and did not find what they suspected for the second time, so we all breathed a sigh of relief.

Wednesday, June 10, 2020, that same doctor called again and started with your mother is very sick. He explained that they did not find what was wrong, other than her having an infection they had been treating, but she was not responding to the medication. He did provide options; however, he said she might not make it through the surgery. Even if she did, most people who survived the surgery only live another three months, maybe. He offered to give me a moment to collect myself and offered to hold a family meeting so he could explain everything to them. I agreed to the meeting, we scheduled it and ended the conversation.

Thursday, June 11, 2020 – was the family meeting. This meeting was hard, I imagine, for everyone, but it was apparent my brother wanted to hold on longer. He wanted to hear more reasons why there was nothing else they could do. My mom's sisters were on the phone as well, and they were saying she has been through enough, but it's up to you guys. We ultimately decided to put my mother in hospice. We needed to find a place that would allow us to visit her, remember we were in the middle of COVID 19. Although we were putting her in hospice, They explained that she might not make more than a day or two. My aunts who live out of town asked if we could move her on Saturday so they could have time to get here.

Friday, June 12, 2020
Our Last conversation! In the end, my mother was not very alert and didn't appear to know what was going on. However, the Friday before she passed away, we had many conversations. It became clear to me that she was aware of what was happening. I am the oldest child and the one with medical power of attorney. My mother asked me if I had spoken to my brother about what the doctor and I had discussed. To test her awareness, I said, what do you think

the doctor and I discussed? She said, about me going to the other hospital! She went on to say, "they said they could make me comfortable, and I think it's time!" At that moment, I lost it. I had to put the phone on mute as she talked because I did not want to upset her. She went on to say, "Angela, please help your sister," and began to tell me about a situation my sister was in that I was not aware of… I will not share that as it is personal to her, but I am here for her when she is ready. As I mentioned earlier, I had just started a new job, so I was at work on this particular day in my office with a coworker. At that moment, I could not concern myself with who was around; it just was what it was. I do not remember how the conversation ended, but we talked several times that day. I think she was aware of what was happening, and she wanted to talk to us, so she called a lot. My youngest brother was having a hard time handling it; I called my other brother to speak to him about it, he told me he knew, then went on to say I told him to please talk to her.

My mom has been gone seven months, one week, three days, and three hours at this writing. She has been on my heart heavy for the past two weeks; every day, I have thought of her. I have not had that happen since she first passed away. I have heard many people say, "not a day goes by that I have not thought of my mother," and I would wonder what is wrong with me that I have had plenty of days I had not thought of my mom or at least consciously. If I am honest, I think I have blocked many of those thoughts. There was some temptation to feel bad about that, but I can't, and I will not judge myself. It's not that I do not want to think of my mom, but it hurts too much to remember that she is not here with me.

Chapter 5

I thought we had more time!

My mother had been through a lot, she had a few stays in a nursing home for rehabilitation, but this last stay seemed to be getting to her. She had been in the nursing home this time for over a year. I started to notice that she was becoming depressed and did not seem to be herself. I went to one of my sisters and said, "We need to think about if we are going to let mama spend her last days in a nursing home" I, of course, had no idea this was her last year. We both agreed that we did not want that for her. Although we had our places, we decided to move together because we knew that it would require a lot and we could not do it alone.

I wanted to wait to tell my mom until we found a place, but my sister told her that we had decided to find a place and get her out of the nursing home. That was the best decision in hindsight because almost immediately, we could see a difference in her. She was no longer depressed. She got involved in nearly every part of the process. When we looked at houses, she was on facetime saying, let me see this room, how many stairs to get in the house and does that refrigerator make ice. It took us a while, but we finally found a place big enough to accommodate all of us. We moved into the house in late December, but my mother did not move in until early January. My sister picked her up from the nursing facility to bring her home. She shared that they were driving down the street, and all of a sudden, my mother screamed," Oooohhh," which startled her, and when she asked my mom what was wrong, she said, "I'M FREE."

I'm not going to lie; having my mother home was no cakewalk. My sister worked nights and was planning to be home with her during the day but, shortly after we moved together, she was offered a promotion that would put her on the day shift. I was in school full time and raising two children. We made it work. I got up early every morning to cook and make sure she had something to eat. My sister helped with changing bandages when needed (I did not have the stomach to do it). My girls kept her company, made quick meals, and helped with little things. My other siblings and my niece came over to help as well. My mother loved her family, and nothing made her happier than having us all together. We had many family dinners, most of the time, we were not all here simultaneously, but she saw everyone, which made her happy. My brothers spoiled my mother; if she wanted or needed anything, all she had to do was say it. They may not have gone to the store to get it, but they came with the money. My mother had her struggles, but I believe she was happy. She got to spend more time with her children and grandchildren.

My mother loved to sit on the front porch and enjoy the air, we did not have a porch for that, but on Memorial Day, she did have an opportunity to go in the backyard and relax and enjoy time with her family. We didn't know that was the last holiday we would have with her.

Life is so unpredictable; it never crossed my mind that my mother would be leaving so soon. Over the years, I noticed her doing less but did not understand it was due to a combination of her getting older and her medical conditions. In hindsight, I can see how she was lonely; she called me several times a day to talk about nothing in particular. I spoke with her almost every time, although there were times that I got frustrated because she had forgotten that I was at work or school. There were also times when we would spend family time together, and I would be on my laptop doing schoolwork or some other project I wanted to get done. I spent that time "multitasking" instead of being in the moment and just enjoying the time. Being a member of the sandwich generation is hard. Those unfamiliar with the term sandwich generation are people raising children and caring for aging parents who need their help. Making things even more complicated, I went back to school, spreading myself even thinner. In life, we are faced with many decisions, but I have learned that one decision we must make is being present in our time with loved ones cherish that time while you have it.

    I knew my mother was getting older, but she was only 64, I knew she had some medical concerns, but she had bounced back so many times. My mother lived six months after we moved her out of the nursing home. I am genuinely grateful that we were able to spend that time with her. This loss was shocking and devastating to all my mother's children, grandchildren, siblings, nieces, nephews, and friends. We thought we had more time.

Chapter 6

The Year of First

Services
June 23, 2020 –

Waking up this morning knowing it would be my last time seeing my mother felt overwhelming, but I had to be strong for my daughters and siblings. My girls and I had hair appointments that morning, so we were out early. My stylist had recently lost her mother. When we began talking, I felt comforted. It was not anything that she said; it was the connection of hearts. My father and stepmother called me that morning to see how I was doing. I had not spoken with them since my mom passed away. It was good to hear their voices.

I headed home to get dressed for the services. I was nervous, almost shaking. My mind is wandering all over the place because every time the thought of saying goodbye comes to mind, I try to think of something else. I get home, and my sisters are in the house getting ready but not dressed. I get dressed and walk out into the living room to realize they still are not dressed. At this point, I am heading to the funeral home alone to approve my mother's body. My heart is heavy, I am not ready, but there is no more time.

I walked out of the door to leave, and one of my best friends, Terry, was taking things out of her car to drop off at the house. I felt a rush of emotion come over me. I could no longer hold it in. When I saw her, I felt safe because I knew she would be there for me. She walked over to the car to hug me and asked where I was headed. When I responded that I was going to the funeral home, she said I'm coming with you. I will follow you. It meant the world to me that she was there.

Although we were in the middle of Covid 19, many people showed up to provide support, and I truly appreciated each one of them. As if the funeral and saying goodbye to my mother was not hard enough, there was a substantial chaotic scene right in the middle of everything. I will not be sharing the detail of that in this book. I only mention it because I could not believe the lack of respect for my mother. Once the commotion calmed slightly, I went to my mother's casket and envisioned her disappointment. I could hear her voice and see the look on her face that usually let you know she was unhappy. I could not help but break down because my mother did not deserve that, we were here to honor her, and all involved parties allowed it to become about something else.

July 5, 2020

    I set the writing aside for a minute. I am now at week three since my mother left this earth. I still cannot sleep. I have started to surround myself with pillows for comfort. Unfortunately, it has not gotten any easier. I feel as though I am living in a fog. I do not know how I am making it through each day. My habit has been to avoid the sad feelings and push them aside. I know that is not good for me, but I am concerned about wants on the other side of that door. As much as I hurt now, I fear the pain of letting that door open completely.

July 10, 2020

Today started as a typical workday; I was leaving one client's home and getting ready to head to the next when I noticed a missed call from the funeral home. My heart immediately sank as I thought to myself, I wish I had not seen that. All kinds of thoughts started running through my mind, like, I'm not sure if I am ready for this. Something in me just knew that I would need to be the one to deal with this, but do I go alone? Should I ask one of my friends to go with me? For a moment, I allowed myself to wonder what they might want. However, I knew the only thing they could be calling me for was to tell me that the cremains was ready to be picked up. I called my brother and confessed that I had not called them back but was not sure I was ready; his response was, well, they will wait until you are ready; they will be ok. This confirmed what I already knew. I must be the one to do this. I did not bother to call them back. Of course, they called again that Monday, July 13. I finally returned the call that Wednesday, July 15, hoping they would give me until the weekend to come in because I did not know how this process would affect me.

July 18, 2020

    I got up early and had breakfast with a friend, and during breakfast, I asked her to go with me to pick up my mother's cremains. I am grateful that she agreed; I do not think I would have gotten through that alone. Walking into that funeral home was so surreal. Other families were waiting to meet with the director, and I recalled sitting in their seats. There were people there attending services for their loved ones, and I remembered seeing my mother for the last time. I was fidgeting, getting up from my seat, walking around, then sitting down trying to make conversation with my friend. Finally, the funeral director came out, and I asked her if she would fill the necklaces for my sibling and me. She agreed, and I sat down again to wait. She came back a few moments later to get me and took me to a room where she had the jewelry on the desk placed on a paper towel next to this box with my mother's name on it. To be honest, I do not remember anything she said to me. I just remember sitting there looking at this box of ashes that is my mother's body.

August 13, 2020

As we have finished up this graduation season, I am saddened because much of it reminds me of my mother. My mother would have been so proud of her granddaughter. Although we were in the middle of Covid 19, and the graduation was virtual, she would have been right in front of the television. As we were planning for the truck party, and I was taking things off the list because I didn't think we needed it, I could hear her saying, "Angie, you know you can get that for my baby," followed by "how much is it." When we left to take Jayla to school, I was reminded of road trips with my mom. We always had great road trips; we talked about any and everything. When I started driving, I thought about how my mother would have figured out a way to be in that car to drop her baby off.

As I was driving, the girls fell asleep, and I was listening to music. I remembered that a good friend called me after my mom passed and left me a message to call her. I had not gotten around to returning the call. Honestly, I had not called her because she is one of those people that draws you in like a magnet. Her loving spirit, uplifting and kind words, in addition to her ability to listen, pulls you in. I knew if I called, I would have to face emotions that I did not think I was ready for. As I drove, I thought, "I'm in a good place emotionally I can handle calling her." I called my friend Claudia Dancy-Davis, and we chatted for a while. Then she began telling me she lost her mom; my heart sank as she told me about the circumstances that took her mother. Claudia began to tell me about her last conversations with her mom. In one conversation, in particular, her mother kept telling her she was sick, and she would say, no, mom, I am fine. After her mom passed away, Claudia went to the doctor and learned she was sick, and at the time of our conversation, she wasn't sure of the prognosis. I began to ask about the treatment plan and other questions; she was gracious and answered my questions. Claudia then said to me; I wanted you to call me because I wanted to let you know that I appreciate your friendship. I also wanted to tell you that you are doing a great job raising your girls. You are an excellent example for them in many ways, including going back to school and getting your MSW. Lastly, she said I did not want to leave this earth without telling you these things and making sure you knew I appreciated you. I was utterly speechless; I had to mute the phone because I had lost it. I just could not control my emotions. I could not pull myself together enough to talk, much less figure out what to say. I do not remember now how we ended the conversation, but I'm sure I said something. I cried the rest of the drive to East St. Louis. I was thinking about my mom and the last conversation with her. I was thinking about how she was not here anymore and that I was on this road trip without her.

I am grateful for my aunts Shirley Peterson and Dorothy McKinney, who stood in the gap and took a trip to Jackson, Mississippi. One was with me to drop Jayla off, and the other one went with me when I picked her up. As we drove down, we talked about many things, including memories of my mother.

October 15, 2020

I made it through my mom's birthday without her for the first time a few days ago, and I will say it was a challenge. The closer we got to her birthday, the more emotional I got. Then, of course, my sister Syrennia planned this big celebration. I was not sure I was even in the mood for that; I wanted to be alone. So I got up early on her birthday, got dressed then left the house. The pain of not having her here was nearly unbearable; I do not remember what I did, but I eventually came home and joined the celebration.

    The celebration was bittersweet for other reasons as well. Days before My moms' birthday, there was a rift in the relationship between her children, and I honestly do not think things will ever be the same, but time will tell.

My birthday - November 6, 2020

    I am grateful for this day! Although I am grateful, it has been a challenge, waiting for a call I will never get again. I had my break down early this morning. I was not expecting this to be this hard and tied to suppress it. I got many texts and Facebook posts and responded to what I could. The angels always take care of me. One of my early morning texts came from a friend Gail Myer saying, "happy birthday, and I know this day is hard." My heart was comforted because someone understood what I was feeling. I was born at 5:21 pm and had mentioned it to a friend and coworker. The closer I got to that time, the more emotional I became. I was trying to hold it in, and precisely at 5:21 pm, my friend Tadora Hull texted me. My heart was comforted, but I could no longer hold my emotions. I spent the next several minutes crying uncontrollably. I just kept thinking that without her, there would be no me, and she is not here. Grief is complicated! There are no shortcuts; you just get through it. Although, at times, it does not feel like I will make it.

I came home, and my amazing daughters showered me with gifts, and my sisters had planned a nice dinner for me. I miss my mom every day, but some days are just awful. Thank you to my BFF Bianca McAtee Thompson for

Running around the city with me all day to keep me busy meant more to me than she would ever know.

February 6, 2021 –

    Dear mommy,

    I have not written you a letter in a while, so I thought it was time. There are so many things I want to tell you, and I am not even sure how. I am grateful for so many things, one of which is you being my mother. Some of my earliest memories are of us talking about any and everything. You were always so open about your experiences, perhaps in hopes that I could learn from your life decisions.

Today is hard because we cannot talk anymore, I am in the last semester of my MSW program, and you will not be here to see me graduate. However, I know you are proud.

May 9, 2021 - Mother's Day

> There are just no words! I spent the day trying to hold myself together, trying to balance my struggle of not having my mom, and trying not to take the day away from girls who had bought gifts to celebrate me.

May 12, 2021

The night before the MSW Graduation, we had our social work department celebration. Due to Covid 19, it was a virtual celebration. The professors all took turns giving us words of wisdom. Then they had us recite the CSU oath of social work. I felt a sense of pride through everything I finished. Next, they showed us a slide show with all the graduates' pictures and music playing in the background. As my picture flashed across the screen, I was overcome with emotion and began to cry. It got so bad that I had to shut off my camera to pull myself together. I could just picture my mom sitting next to me, smiling from ear to ear. I could hear her bragging to her sisters and friends about her baby, who graduated with her MSW. The reality is she is not here, and I will not get to see that smile or listen to her telling everyone. When I got back on camera, it was time for us to have someone pin us with the MSW alumni pin. I was able to hold it together as Jasmine came into the room to pin me.

June 13, 2021

It was around the time I saw her alive for the last time. I remember we had family here in town. They were only allowing two people to visit her every 12 hours. That morning, my aunt Peaches and my sister Sierra went up to see my mom; first, she had just gotten to the hospice location, and they were still trying to get her settled. My sister called me because my mom was in so much pain and screaming for the nurse. I could hear her in the background. That night, we put together the visit schedule, and my cousin and I got to go that night.

I walked in and saw her lying there, all swollen. I had not seen her since Memorial Day, I called her a few times, but she did not respond. I sat in the chair across from her, looking at how swollen she was, and I remember thinking that she would not make it for long. Finally, after sitting for a while, I got up, walked to her bedside, and kissed her on the cheek. Good Night, Mom!

Chapter 7

First Anniversary

As we are approaching the first anniversary of her passing, I find it incredibly painful. Last night I relived the worst moment in my life by far. I dreamt of getting that call all over again that she was no longer with us physically. Maybe I should not have been surprised as I laid in my bed the night before. My heart ached; I felt physical pain in my chest as I thought about her being gone. At times I had to remind myself to breathe. I do not believe there is a cure for this. I must learn to live with it, which could mean something different as the days, weeks, months, and years go by.

These last couple of weeks, I have realized that I have been in a state of denial, Not denying that she is gone but avoiding the whole thing altogether. The pain of her not being here was too much for me to handle all at one time.

As I think about the sayings I have heard for years that seemed like a cliché, boy do I understand the meaning now. As I heard people say that no one will ever love you like your mother, I am reminded of how she became pregnant with me at 15. There were other options, but she chose me. Although, she had no help because my father made a different choice. I am reminded of another time that she chose my brother and me when she could have walked away. Instead, while grieving the loss of her daughter DCFS took us from her, and she decided to fight for us. I do not know what they required of her exactly, but as a DCFS investor now myself, I know the difficulty of that task in general.

As I think about the saying cherish your mother while she is here on this earth, I am ever so grateful that I could do that. But, of course, there are still things I wish I'd done, still things I wish I'd said, but I have no regrets.

June 14, 2021

I do not know how I have done it, but it has been a whole year. I recently realized I have just spent this entire year avoiding many thoughts and just about every conversation that I did not initiate. I was afraid for this day to come because leading up to it was awful. I was not sure what to expect; part of me wanted to go to work and just be busy. The problem with that is I did not know if I could do it emotionally. I think all my siblings were in the same boat; they kept trying to plan something but to my knowledge, I do not think they moved on anything.

We got a group text from Jayla a few days before saying, don't worry about anything, just be here at 5:15 pm. her grandchildren made plans for how she would be celebrated today.

When I got home, there were so many people in the yard, family and friends who came to celebrate with us. When I got out of the car, I could see the decoration on the porch and realized that this was a more significant celebration than I thought. I later learned that her grandchildren (Lamarre'l Barber 19, Jayla Barber 18, Kevin Barber Jr 17. and Jasmine Barber 15) planned the whole thing. They paid for everything (decorations, food, drinks, and balloons to release). They reached out to other family members and invited them to come and asked them to help with cooking the dishes they did not cook themselves. I did not ask, but there was a feeling that the intent was to honor their grandmother and her children. I could not be prouder of them, and I know she had the biggest smile on her face as she was looking down. This is an example of the love she showed them and the selfless example she set for them. We love you and miss you more than words could ever express.

September 9, 2021

    Dear Mom, it has been over a year, and it is still a struggle. However, I am making it through little by little. I just got home a few days ago from my weekend getaway to East St. Louis. There were several moments during my trip that I thought of you. On the drive down, I thought about the many trips we took traveling to visit the family. The long talks we would have about any and everything, the times you would fall asleep on me as I drove. I thought about how you loved taking those trips visiting family. Even as I type this, I could just see you sitting at the end of the table at Aunt Shirley's house asking, "what you cook?" I can hear you laughing at all the crazy things that would happen or crazy conversations. As much as it makes me feel sad and brings tears to my eyes, I fear that one day I will not be able to recall your voice or hear you laughing in my mind, and that makes me sadder.

I will keep working through this as I must, but I do wish you were here.

    I wanted to let you know that I am just about done with the book, and I will publish it on your birthday, 10/11/21. There is no doubt in my mind that you are proud.

Chapter 8

Living with Grief

Grief is personal and depends on a lot of different factors. When my mom passed away, it was hard to find comfort. Everyone you can imagine is there to check on you and see if you need anything before the service, even on the day of service. Once services are over, they go back to their lives, and many expect you to do the same. The calls stopped, and I felt like I had no one to talk to about my feelings after a while. I was out with friends one evening, and they asked how I had been doing. As I began to tell them I started tearing up, one of them immediately asked the other to show her to the restroom, they both walked away. When they came back, we just started to talk about other things. I never asked, but I guess they were uncomfortable with me tearing up.

One thing that gave me comfort was to write, so that is what I did.

Sometimes I wrote letters to my mom; other times, I wrote how I was feeling in the moment. I found comfort in talking with those who lost a parent because they understood what I was going through. I could talk to them about things that would not make sense to others. If I began to tear up, they understood and continued to listen without making me feel like something was wrong with me. I did eventually learn that everyone who loses parents does not necessarily feel the same way about it. In a conversation with one of my professors from the MSW program I recently completed, we talked about how grief will depend on many different variables. Who you lost, your relationship with the person, their age at death, and the way they died.

Grieving is a process, and that process is going to be different as well. To me, grief does not just go away. You learn to live with it. Each day without your loved one becomes just a little easier, although it initially does not feel like it. In the beginning. I developed different habits that, for a time, helped me get through the pain. As mentioned earlier, I could not sleep, so I would drink a few sips of Grand Marnier. For some, this may not seem like a lot, but this was not my prior habit. I went to the boat several times a week because I could not stand being in the house. These were the habits that I felt, if left unchecked, could become self-destructive behaviors. Although I had people around me, I felt alone; I felt like I just needed a hug sometimes. When I went to bed at night, I started to put one pillow close behind my back and one close to the front of my body that I would hold on to, in addition to the one I had under my head. This became my security.

Acknowledgments

Jayla, I remember the day you came to live with me; I was nervous and excited at the same time. I was a young single woman who until then had only been responsible for myself. I wanted to do everything just perfectly, all the things they say you should do in books. I read and sang to you every single night before I put you to bed. I'm sure you have no memory of those days. I am so proud of you, and every day you make me prouder. I cannot wait to see what you will become; I am amazed at your organization and discipline. We are at the transition stage of our relationship, the stage where I must learn to let go, pray and trust that you have learned the things that I have tried to teach you. Yet, at the same time, define, deepen and transition to a mother-daughter friendship.

Jasmine, I remember the first time I saw you; you were just a little over 2 pounds. I was so afraid to hold you, but when I did, I fell in love. I was told you would need to stay in the hospital for about another month or so. So I went to work and filled out my FMLA papers and started visiting you every day. I sang to you, read books to you, feed you, and then sat and held you until it was time for me to pick your sister up from school. When you came home, I was super excited and could not wait for you to meet your sister and the rest of the family. I am proud of you; you have so many natural talents that I can hardly keep up. My goal has been to allow you the room and opportunity to cultivate those talents to see which you want to pursue long term. I am excited to see what you will decide. You are still in high school at the writing of this book and growing so fast.

Girls, life is going to hand you some difficult blows, but you can get

through it. Keep putting one foot in front of the other, and you will get there. Although finding the love of your life may lead you to heartbreak first, know that you will heal. One day should you decide, you will have children of your own, which will have a set of challenges, but you can do it. As I write this, I wonder if sharing my hurt with you guys could help, but honestly, I do not know-how. I have always been one to suffer alone, there have been rare moments when I have shown emotion in front of others, but those times were few. Know that I am proud of you. I could not have asked for better daughters. Although you did not come from my body, know that I could not have loved you more. Always hold on to each other, love each other and let nothing come between you.
Although I hope I have at least another 30 years, we just cannot be sure. Know that while I am on this earth, I will always be your biggest cheerleader and, at times, your harshest critic, but that is because I love you so much.

Thank you to my family, my siblings (my mother's children). I was not sure how we would deal with this as a unit, but I think mom would be proud. We became closer than I could have imagined. I am praying that we can keep a close relationship and be there for each other. I know this year has been just as hard for you. Siblings on my father's side, thank you for the calls and text of condolence.

Thank you to my aunts and uncle, who was my rock, helping me through this challenging process. Talking to me and advising me through the process, although you were struggling yourself, having lost your sister. I am grateful to each of you.

Thank you to my cousins, who were there for their parents as they prepared to say goodbye to their sister. Thank you to my cousin Antonio Barber who did not make it to the funeral but came a few weeks later to check in on us and hang out. Thank you to my cousin Cynthia Danley; I struggle to find words that adequately express my gratitude for her support. She was by my side the whole time (sometimes physically, sometimes in spirit). She was with me when I got the horrible news and stayed with me during the service. When others showed up to provide support, she fell back, allowing space, but I knew she was only steps away. I could never repay her for that.

Thank you to my close friends, I have many friends, but for this book, I will only mention those that stood out specifically for this situation. If I forget anyone, please charge it to my head and not my heart.

In no particular order, thank you to India Gray-Schmiedlin. Who talked to me every day while my mother was in the hospital, encouraging me, listening to me, and offering advice when requested. She also provided support once my mother passed. She listened and honestly said, "Angie, I wish I knew what to say to you. I wish that I could help; if you need anything, I'm here".

Thank you to Bianca McAtee-Thompson, who was also there to listen every day. If I needed to get out of the house, she was there. This first year has been challenging, and she was there. In addition, Bianca made herself available for all the holidays and birthdays to hang out, making these more manageable for me.

Thank you to Precious Conner, who came to the service to provide support and later went with me to the funeral home when I picked up my mother's cremains.

Thank you to Kendra Jackson-Freeman, who called to offer condolences and asked, "what day are you available for me to drop off dinner;" what do the girls like. I appreciated this more than she could know. I never understood the concept of taking food to people until then. My mind was all over the place, and I did not think having someone bring dinner was a huge help. When she came over, she sat for a while, and we just talked, which was also appreciated.

Thank you to Tasha Fletcher, a dear friend I had not spoken with in a while who just showed up at the service for my mother. That meant the world to me. There is a saying that "Friends are like stars, you don't always see them, but you know that they are there."

Thank you to Terry London; she is one of the people I would not have made it without. On the day of services, I walked out of the house headed to the funeral home alone when she pulled up. I was so overwhelmed with emotion when I saw her I had a breakdown. She followed me to the funeral home and was with me when I saw my mother for the first time at the funeral home. Needless to say, that initial viewing was challenging. I do not remember what she was doing, but she did not notice that I had walked out of the funeral home because I was starting to become emotional standing there looking at my mother. Before long, she came rushing out behind me to provide comfort as I tried to pull myself together.

My mother's dear friends also supported Donna Reeves, Juanita Lyons, Aisha Muhammad, and Mary Anderson. Thank you so much! We love and appreciate you.

So many others reached out to provide support, but I could never mention you all. Know that we appreciate every gesture.

About the Author

Angela Renee' Barber, MSW

Angela Barber is an International Best-Selling Author, Certified Professional Life Coach, Entrepreneur, Motivational Speaker, and a Child Protection Investigator for IDCFS.

Angela has been working as a social work professional for the last 19 years. She has been a strong advocate for foster families by serving on the Statewide Foster Care Advisory Council for seven years includes the two years she served as chair. In addition, she worked as an independent contractor as a Lead foster parent support specialist. In 2007 Angela was recognized by the National Association of Black Social Workers for her commitment to children. In addition, she was nominated for the Ruth Massinger award in 2008 for her work as a foster parent. Angela also advocated for birth families and youth in care. In her work with Strengthening Families of Illinois, she focused on building leadership among foster parents, birth parents, and teens aging out of foster care.

As a coach, she primarily works with people looking for help navigating through their grief, offering both one-on-one and group sessions. In addition, Angela has had speaking engagements as an independent contractor with IDCFS, Strengthening Families of Illinois, and community organizations.

Angela has also worked with community organizations to enhance the quality of life of those in the community. For example, she worked as an Administrative Coordinator on the Neighborhood Recovery Initiative (NRI) for the Greater Auburn Gresham Development Corporation. In this work, Angela focused on providing employment to parents and training them to be leaders in their community. She also interned with the Chicago Area Project (CAPS), assisting with the "Most Youth Don't Use" campaign, focusing on decreasing the number of youth abusing drugs and alcohol.

Angela decided to pursue higher education later in life while being a single parent to her two girls, who were 12 and 9 years old at the time, and being an entrepreneur. She graduated with Honors in 2018, received her Bachelors in Sociology, then graduating 2021 with her Master of Social Work degree. Angela lives in Chicago, Illinois, with her two daughters Jayla 19, and Jasmine, 16. She enjoys road trips, sitting at the lake, enjoying nature, and spending time with family and friends.

Reach the Author

Angela Barber
Email: barber@livingwithgrief.com
Facebook: **AB-Elevation - Grief Coach**

Services offered
Grief support groups
Individual Grief coaching

Additional Book
Co-Author of Letters To My Little Sister
(contact to purchase)

www.ingramcontent.com/pod-product-compliance
Lightning Source LLC
LaVergne TN
LVHW051506070426
835507LV00022B/2956